PRAYING THROUGH CANCER

28 Days of Prayer

Todd Outcalt

UPPER ROOM BOOKS®
NASHVILLE

Cover image: Shutterstock / www.shutterstock.com
Cover design: Left Coast Design / www.lcoast.com

Library of Congress Cataloging-in-Publication Data

Names: Outcalt, Todd.
Title: Praying through cancer : 28 days of prayer / Todd Outcalt.
Description: Nashville, TN : Upper Room Books, [2016]
Identifiers: LCCN 2016006536| ISBN 9780835815758 (print) | ISBN 9780835815765 (mobi) | ISBN 9780835815772 (epub)
Subjects: LCSH: Cancer—Patients—Prayer-books and devotions—English.
Classification: LCC BV4910.33 .O93 2016 | DDC 242/.86196994—dc23
LC record available at http://lccn.loc.gov/2016006536

To the Calvary "Prayer Warriors"

*Be alert and always keep on praying for
all the Lord's people.*

—Ephesians 6:18, NIV

CONTENTS

ACKNOWLEDGMENTS

Every book is a product of relationships, love, and experiences. This is especially true for this prayer guide, and I would like to thank the many friends (and, in some cases, families) who have shared their lives and stories with me. I also thank Upper Room Books—a ministry of resources and people that reaches around the world. And, as always, I thank my family for providing a small space to work and a larger space for love and laughter. My wife, Becky, continues to inspire me every day, and I thank her for sharing her cancer journey with me and with others.

INTRODUCTION

In many ways, this is a very personal book. My wife is a fourteen-year breast cancer survivor, and as a pastor of thirty-five years, I have known hundreds of people who have made their own cancer journeys. Many are alive and still telling their stories; others are with the Lord.

My intent in writing this book is twofold. First, I hope to give cancer patients (and their families) a practical tool for prayer, reflection, and devotion over a four-week period. A month can be a significant chunk of time for someone diagnosed with cancer, and I hope this book provides a brief encounter with God—a promise, a testimony, a prayer—that lifts the spirit and enlivens the heart with courage and faith.

Second, I hope this book will kick-start some of the questions that all cancer patients eventually ask themselves: *What does this experience mean? How will cancer change me? What is my purpose? What can I learn from this experience? What can I offer to others through this experience?*

Although this book serves as a personal prayer guide, I trust that the daily Bible readings and reflection questions will make family conversation or group study possible. Cancer support groups may find this guide to be a helpful tool, and I hope this book finds its way to those shelters of mercy.

I feel humbled that those who have completed their cancer journeys have shared their thoughts and experiences with me. I pray that every reader will find this guide to be accessible, honest, and uplifting. And in the end, I trust that God will be honored as the Giver of all good things.

HOW TO USE THIS BOOK

This book contains a series of daily Bible readings and personal reflections. Start with day one—regardless of where you are in your cancer journey (change the numbers in the book if you need to). I believe you will find a relevance to the readings no matter where your treatments fall and regardless of the decisions you are making.

Begin by reading the Bible passage for the day, along with the daily verse. Take a moment to reflect on the scripture reading, and then read the devotion. Afterward, pray the day's prayer, adding to it from your own life and concerns as appropriate. Use the questions at the back of the book as additional tools for reflection and prayer each week. These questions may also be used in a small-group setting.

WEEK 1

Speaking of Cancer & Overcoming Shock

MONDAY
Why me?

Read Psalm 88.

> *O LORD, God of my salvation,*
> *when, at night, I cry out in your presence,*
> *let my prayer come before you;*
> *incline your ear to my cry.*

> —Psalm 88:1-2

The first question my wife asked when she was diagnosed with breast cancer was, "Why me?" This was not so much a theological question as an emotional one—a question that helped her process the shock of her cancer diagnosis. *Cancer*, after all, is a scary word. The word evokes many images and ideas, and most people struggle in coming to terms with a cancer diagnosis.

Disbelief, shock, pain, isolation—all of these feelings and more are normal responses to cancer. In fact, I can't think of a *wrong* response to cancer. Every person will respond differently. And every journey through cancer will be unique. But as this prayer guide will show, you will discover that your initial responses to cancer will morph into new forms of strength and hope. You will discover that prayer encourages you in amazing ways. You will find support in family and friends.

In my thirty-five years of pastoral work, I have seen these truths played out in hundreds of lives. Whether breast cancer, lung cancer, or any other form, cancer provokes a rallying cry of faith that lifts people toward grace and emboldens them to ask questions, seek help, and find support in amazing places. If you are in the early stages of your cancer journey, don't doubt that you will discover new sources of strength as well.

Keep asking questions. Keep seeking. And you will find hope in God's amazing grace.

Early in my wife's journey, as she struggled to make sense of the disease that had invaded her body, she initially withdrew from others—even those closest to her—and grew despondent. But as she talked with other breast cancer survivors, read literature about cancer, and began having conversations with her doctors, she became energized by hope. She allowed others to help her. She learned how to receive support. And in time, she had made her treatment plan, and she felt empowered to live with her decisions. Through surgery, chemotherapy, and recovery, my wife made the journey toward healing. But her journey began with hope.

As you consider your initial reactions to your diagnosis, don't forget that others have walked the path laid out before you. Own your feelings but remember this: You are not alone. As you think about your support team, your family, and your friends, begin by asking yourself this set of questions: *What would be helpful to me? What do I need from my friends and family? What do I need from God?*

As you ask these questions and others, I encourage you to pray. Your prayers don't need to be elaborate to be helpful. Let them be truthful; let them come from the heart.

Prayer

God, I am hurting. I am afraid. I have so many questions, and I don't know the answers. I don't know what decisions I should make. But I know that I need your help to make this journey. Help me to reach out to you and to those who love me. Through it all, I will, by your grace, find the strength to hope in you. Amen.

TUESDAY
Say the word

Read Psalm 103:1-5.

> *Bless the LORD, O my soul,*
> *and all that is within me,*
> *bless his holy name.*

—Psalm 103:1

In the ancient world, spoken words carried power. Covenants, for example, were expressed verbally, and a person's word was regarded as legally binding, especially in the company of witnesses. Curses were also powerful forces, and the commandment prohibiting the use of God's name in vain reflects the power of God's name to both curse and bless. Likewise, naming children at birth, blessing a firstborn, and passing along a last will and testament were all regarded as powerful words.

Today, although spoken words do not always carry the same weight, words have the power to hurt, heal, and threaten. Certain words, in fact, still have the power to instill fear and anxiety.

One of those words, of course, is *cancer.*

Many cancer patients can recall the date and time when they first heard the words, "You have cancer." They can remember how they felt, how their heart skipped a beat, and how they refused to accept the diagnosis. Perhaps they responded, "There must be some mistake." The C-word certainly holds power.

But as people of faith, other words hold even greater power. Words like *hope, faith, love, prayer, care,* and *family* hold deep significance, and many cancer patients will admit that these other powerful words offered strength as they learned more about their diagnosis and began forming their plans for treatment and support. Yes, words hold power.

Don't be afraid to speak the C-word aloud, but add new words to your vocabulary as well. Words of love, appreciation, gratitude, and need are useful. Bring them along on your journey. Expressing the highest aspirations for your life provides a starting point for bringing these blessings into being. I'm not offering a magical formula for healing, but speaking aloud what you feel, what you want, what you need, and what you hope for offers opportunity for your mental, emotional, and spiritual survival.

Make your list of powerful words, and speak them often. Use positive, encouraging, and hopeful words, and ask your loved ones to do the same. They will change your experience with the C-word. They will change your life.

Prayer

Gracious and loving God, so many words race through my mind. I must confess that I feel fear, anxiety, heartache, and even uncertainty. Help me find encouragement in the vocabulary of faith, hope, and joy. Grant me the peace of knowing that you are with me through these troubles and that I am loved and cared for by many. I will seek encouraging words, and I will use them daily. May they bless me. Amen.

WEDNESDAY
Truth is freedom

Read Ephesians 5:6-14.

For once you were darkness, but now in the Lord you are light. Live as children of light—for the fruit of the light is found in all that is good and right and true. Try to find out what is pleasing to the Lord.

—Ephesians 5:8-10

One of the most difficult aspects of a cancer diagnosis is truth—or, more specifically, the desire on the part of the patient to avoid the whole truth of the disease. Often, patients don't want to know the facts, or they hope that the doctor will sugarcoat the diagnosis and tell them what they want to hear.

I have seen this approach many times in cancer patients, and they struggle in hearing the truth from doctors or from family members who wish to speak truth in love. But as Jesus says, "You will know the truth, and the truth will make you free" (John 8:32).

Likewise, the cancer journey is, if anything, a pilgrimage toward truth. In fact, cancer patients must live in the truth of their diagnosis if they are to make the journey toward wholeness. Hiding in half-truths, refusing to speak of the disease, or pretending that all is well does not provide the support, hope, or faith necessary to make the arduous trek toward healing. Truth provides freedom.

I have learned this lesson through other situations in my life. Many times, over the course of my thirty-two-year marriage, I have shied away from certain truths about myself—my weaknesses, faults, and failures. Sometimes receiving my wife's insights and opinions about my actions was difficult.

But whenever I have been open to the truth, change was not long in coming. Truth allowed me to grow, adapt, and seek the best for others and myself.

As you consider your cancer diagnosis, make a commitment today that you will seek the truth, that you will desire to know all the aspects and intricacies of your treatment and what will be required of you. In doing so, your hope will grow and your resolve will blossom. Embracing this honest approach will fill your heart with amazing insights and enable you to make the decisions that are best for you.

Keep truth at the forefront of your cancer journey. Be open to receiving truth from your doctors, family, support network, and friends. And hold fast to the greatest truth of all: God is with you!

Prayer

God, I don't like to think of myself as a cancer patient. Sometimes I want to pretend that this disease has not invaded my body, that nothing has changed, and that I can continue my life as before. But I am going to accept the truth of my diagnosis and make my journey toward wholeness. I will not shy away from listening, learning, and loving. Be my truth, dear God, and guide me down the path that restores and redeems. To you I offer thanks and praise. Amen.

THURSDAY
Drawing in

Read Psalm 102:1-12.

Hear my prayer, O Lord;
let my cry come to you.
Do not hide your face from me
in the day of my distress.
Incline your ear to me;
answer me speedily in the day when I call.

—Psalm 102:1-2

Many of Jesus' teachings focus on the internal—a person's thoughts and feelings. For example, Jesus teaches that people express real gratitude when they are not concerned with showcasing their generosity. He also teaches that his followers should be the salt of the earth and that private prayers hold more power than public ones. Indeed, as Jesus teaches, his followers are strengthened from the inside out.

Receiving a cancer diagnosis is a traumatic event, and many people respond to the diagnosis by retreating from life and withdrawing from family and friends. Sometimes these actions are necessary—perhaps even essential—so that a person can begin the work of drawing on his or her inner strength, discovering the hope and courage that will be needed in the months ahead.

Like the psalmist's prayer, your prayers will become quite personal—perhaps even urgent. The prayers you offer during the subsequent days after a cancer diagnosis may be filled with questions, pleadings, even distress. But those prayers result from natural emotions, and you may even draw strength from them. In fact, honesty itself makes prayers more powerful, more wonderful, and more personal. And like the psalm-ist, you may ask God to work quickly, to come to your aid now—not later. Cancer brings out this urgency in people's emotions and prayers.

Consider your current needs. In what ways are you draw-ing strength from inside yourself—through your own hon-esty and urgency? And how are you trusting God with your raw emotions and your hopes for the future?

Drawing in can also give you the space to find points of gratitude—feelings of thankfulness for family and friends, opportunities to thank God for growing inner strength. Drawing in is essential for the journey ahead, and you must ground yourself in your internal power before undertaking any arduous task. And cancer, indeed, is arduous.

Take a moment today to reflect on your life: where have you come from, what is happening to you right now, and where do your hopes reside? Take a moment to draw inside, to express your honest feelings to God—the God who loves you, cares for you, and will be your strength and guide.

Prayer

O God, I am afraid. I feel the weight of my diagnosis, uncer-tainty about the future, and confusion about decisions I will need to make. I ask for your guidance. I need you now. Abide with me in the days ahead. Help me find strength in the peo-ple around me, gratitude as I consider my blessings, and hope in every decision. Amen.

FRIDAY
Reaching out

Read Psalm 77:1-14.

*You are the God who works wonders;
    you have displayed your might among the peoples.*

—Psalm 77:14

Some years ago, when my father was having difficulty walking, I gave him a "grabber"—a mechanical extension that he could use from his chair to pick up items from the floor or nearby table. This simple device enabled him to extend his reach during a time when he was immobile. In time, even after his walking improved, he continued to keep the "grabber" by his side. It was a useful tool.

But using that tool did not come easily for my father. At first, he resisted the need for it. Perhaps he had grown accustomed to his own efforts, or perhaps his pride and independence kept him from admitting that he needed it. He did not make an easy transition into a life of requiring help.

The same may hold true for many in the early stages of a cancer diagnosis. Many people are reluctant to reach out for assistance. Perhaps their pride, a strong spirit of independence, or the nagging feeling that they are becoming a burden keeps them from asking for help. But most cancer patients eventually arrive at a place where they need the aid of others.

With cancer, isolation does not bring healing, happiness, or hope. Rather, people find those things after they have reached out for help. But this is not an easy step for many. In a time and a culture that expects independence, individualism, and success through a person's own efforts and hard work, people want to believe that they can make their journeys alone. They don't want to burden others with their hardship. Yet, many cancer patients struggle to keep their independence intact, eventually realizing that others must be invited into their journey toward healing.

As you consider your cancer diagnosis today, take a few moments to give thanks for the people in your life. Aren't these the people who love you, who are willing to come alongside you and assist you in your time of need? Release any feelings of pride, individualism, or guilt that may be holding you back from seeking help. Through others, you may discover a renewed energy and strength.

Extend your reach.

Prayer

Heavenly Father, I know that you have placed other people in my life for such a time as this, and now I need their help. Please help me release the feelings that I am a bother or a burden to those who love me. Allow me to take a step toward deeper community and relationship. I cannot make this journey alone. I need your help and the help of others. Amen.

SATURDAY
Grief is strength

Read Psalm 103:13-16.

As a father has compassion for his children,
so the LORD has compassion for those who fear him.
For he knows how we were made;
he remembers that we are dust.

—Psalm 103:13-14

Throughout my thirty-five years of pastoral ministry, I have had the opportunity and privilege to walk with people through the stages of grief. I learned that grief has many faces, many forms. Grief can be debilitating, but it can also offer a release, a means by which people become empowered, focused, and refreshed. I have seen this many times and also experienced it myself.

Some years ago, for example, I accompanied an older woman who had no family in the area to her first chemotherapy treatment. On the way to the treatment center, the woman broke down and began to sob, her grief spilling over in great waves of anguish. As we talked, I learned that she had much unspoken grief in her life: estranged children, unresolved issues with her deceased husband, and feelings of isolation. But as she spoke of this grief, I could see a new strength—a kind of resolve—that was empowering her.

Suddenly, as we prepared to walk into the treatment center, she wrested herself free of the grief and said, "Well, I can't change the past. I have work to do. This is not what I wanted, but it's what I have. And now I've got to do my best to face this cancer."

I was at once amazed and inspired by her words. Her grief had given way to acceptance, and she faced her chemo treatments with amazing determination and focus. In that moment in the car, I knew she had found the strength she would need for her cancer journey.

But this change came after her grief—a refreshing, cleansing sadness that allowed her to unburden herself and name her past and her fears. Subsequently, she felt empowered to look toward her future.

Today, allow your grief to be your strength. Grief is not a bad emotion—especially if we are open to the acceptance that it brings. As Jesus says, "Blessed are those who mourn, for they will be comforted" (Matt. 5:4).

What comfort do you need from God today? What burdens can you unload? Do you face unresolved issues that you need to release into God's care? Allow God to change your grief into strength.

Prayer

My Helper, thank you for allowing me to lay my burdens before you today. I have many sadnesses in my life; cancer is only one of them. But I know you can change my heart and offer renewal. In my grief, I pray that you will come to my side and strengthen me for the tasks and hurdles ahead. I don't know what tomorrow will bring, but you know. For that reason, I place my life in your hands, O God. Amen.

SUNDAY
Embracing God's strength

Read Psalm 103:17-22.

The steadfast love of the LORD is from everlasting to everlasting.

—Psalm 103:17

A few years ago, my grandmother died only a few months short of her 101st birthday. When my family assembled photographs of her life to display at her funeral, we were inspired by the number of photos that were taken on Sunday mornings with my grandmother dressed in her "Sunday best." My grandmother only ever missed worship if she were sick or traveling. Seeking God remained at the center of her life.

The Psalms recount times of turmoil and trouble, moments when individuals and communities felt vulnerable. These ancient prayers reflect the deep emotions of people in times of need. The Psalms serve to remind you—even compel you—of the importance of seeking God when your body is compromised and your spirit is low.

In the past week, you likely have navigated a myriad of emotions and thoughts in the aftermath of your cancer diagnosis. You probably have sought help from a variety of sources, read books and online articles, and asked for the opinions of others. And, yes, you may have turned to God for help as well.

But make this a day when you not only ask for God's help but also receive God's strength. Allow the God of the universe to be your stability in every time of trouble. Do not fear admitting your doubts, anxieties, and questions. In doing so, you will find yourself relying more and more upon the grace and strength of God.

As you begin this journey filled with God's strength, take these three simple steps:

1. Relax. Set aside a time to be alone with God and rest in God's grace. Be content. Allow yourself to be without deadlines and jobs to accomplish. Meet God in a silent space with a quiet heart. Picture yourself in God's presence, and relax into God's mercy.

2. Rest. If you are seeking God's strength, do not rush to accomplish other tasks. A rested body is an energized body. Be still and allow God to fill you with new energy and hope.

3. Renew. As you seek God today, picture your body being renewed and refreshed. Think soothing thoughts. Eat good foods. Feel new energy for the days ahead.

Prayer

Dear God, I need you now. I need your strength, your grace, and your healing touch. I feel alone and tired, my energies wasted. Renew me and place a right spirit within me. Refresh me through loving thoughts, beautiful expressions, and the highest aspirations of my heart. Do not allow my heart to sink, but lift me with your light and love. Amen.

WEEK 2

Making Decisions & Learning Again

MONDAY
Back to school

Read Proverbs 1:1-7.

Let the wise also hear and gain in learning.

—Proverbs 1:5

Soon after my wife recovered from her mastectomy, she began making plans to continue her education. Her recovery was hastened because she did not need radiation or chemotherapy, for which we were grateful. Being a cancer survivor had changed her perspective on life, and like many others who have experienced trauma, my wife wanted to change careers. She decided to refocus her energies on becoming a teacher. But before she made the decision to go back to school, she spent many hours learning and growing in her understanding of cancer and treatment. She also grew in her faith and her resolve to face her diagnosis with hope and support.

Anyone who has ever received a cancer diagnosis faces many decisions. Some of these decisions come before surgery or treatment, and others after. But wisdom is required for all.

Rest assured, if you are feeling overwhelmed by facts and figures and an overload of information or choices, you are not alone. You may even feel like you have gone back to school.

Or, as the scriptures affirm, you know that you will require wisdom for your journey. Wisdom differs from knowledge. Wisdom is tempered with faith, joy, cooperation, and even the opinions and input of others. Wisdom looks to God for guidance, help, and strength. You obtain knowledge through study and gathering facts that will inform the decisions you need to make. Like wisdom, knowledge grows as you read, listen, ask questions, and expand your field of understanding.

Make today a school day. What do you need to learn? What wisdom might be required in the next week, the next month, or the coming year? Decisions you make today can have a lasting impact on your life.

Wisdom will be your friend as you look to God for answers to your questions and concerns. You may not like the classroom, but the Lord of the universe will guide and teach you.

Prayer

O God, I have so much that I want to know, so much that I want to learn. I feel overwhelmed by all the decisions I need to make—and often I feel alone in my considerations. I may not have all the answers, but I know I will need your strength in the days ahead. Guide me as I begin my journey toward wisdom. Bless me, I pray, in my thoughts and my deliberations. Amen.

TUESDAY
Learning to hope

Read Romans 5:1-11.

Hope does not disappoint us.

—Romans 5:5

Some years ago, a clergy colleague offered me insight about hope. In the months that he cared for his wife, who was suffering with pancreatic cancer, many people dropped by his house to deliver food, express concern, and even to help with household chores. Others dropped by to pray.

At one point, when my friend expressed his hope for his wife's healing, he was met with the admonition that he was holding to a "false hope." Later, as he reflected on this idea, he came to realize that there is no such thing as "false hope." Hope is hope. Hope is never false. It just is.

Regardless of your cancer prognosis, you will be holding on to hope. This hope will offer you a new day, a new outlook, even the ability to enjoy some small part of your days with your family or friends when your energy and mood are at their lowest. Hope is hope.

When the apostle Paul writes to the church at Rome, he encourages the faithful to hold to hope. He writes that hope does not disappoint us, that hope is the active working of our faith within us. In fact, we hope in God. Through hope, we trust in God's grace to see us through difficulties—even tragedies. And though death is the final outcome for everyone, we hold to the hope of a life with God—a life not made with human hands but a life eternal in heaven.

Do some days fill you with dread? Are you experiencing despair? Though these feelings represent natural reactions to the difficulties you are facing, I encourage you to hope. Through hope you will discover that God continues to care for you, that God is with you even—and especially—in the dark times.

Hope is hope. It is never false. Hope is what we live.

Prayer

God, I am thankful that you have given me life, strength, and blessings. When I think of your faithfulness and goodness toward me, hope fills my spirit. I know you will walk with me through the days ahead, and when I enter a dark night of the soul, you will be there to lift me up. Guide me and fill me with hope for the future. Amen.

WEDNESDAY
Leaning on others

Read Ephesians 1:15-23.

I have heard of your faith in the Lord Jesus and your love toward all the saints, and for this reason I do not cease to give thanks for you as I remember you in my prayers.

—Ephesians 1:15-16

Many years ago, I served as a chaplain in a large university hospital. During that time, I helped people from all walks of life and from different faith perspectives. I sat with those who were grieving or questioning.

I recall one particular conversation with a woman named Maisey who was recovering from an automobile accident. Maisey was always alone, and I never saw any visible support network (other than nurses) around her. I asked Maisey if she had family, and she replied, "Most of my family lives out of state, and there is no one close to me." Then she added, "I wish I had someone to lean on."

Many times since that day I have given thanks for having "someone to lean on." Family, friends, a community, a church—the bedrock of my life experiences comprises all these and more. People are not meant to live in solitude—especially when they are hurting or in pain. God created you not only to care for others but also to be cared for.

Any doctor or person in the health industry will confirm that patients who maintain a positive attitude fare better than those with a negative attitude. And likewise patients who are surrounded by the love and support of others fare better than those who are secluded or otherwise alone. Community makes a difference. People need to learn to lean on others.

No doubt you have been considering difficult options for treatment and care, and perhaps you are feeling alone—even if you are surrounded by many loving people. Could offering thanks for the people who are supporting you in your journey provide you with a new perspective? Spend just a few moments praying for these people. Show God your gratitude. Express how much you need these people and how much you appreciate them being in your life.

When my wife and I recently visited Italy, we were fascinated by the many leaning towers that we saw—the one in Pisa being the most famous. These towers seemed to lean on nothing, and yet they were still standing. And then we learned that all these towers had strong foundations. What we could not see—the real strength of these towers—was underground.

The same is true of human relationships. You build your relationship foundations on love and respect and helpfulness—attributes that may go overlooked but that provide strength in time of need. Be thankful for the support in your life, for the foundations that run deep. And learn to lean on others in tough times.

Prayer

Gracious God, I have been the recipient of grace upon grace, including the help from many people in my life. Parents, grandparents, siblings, teachers, coaches, friends, and mentors—all have made an impact on my life. And now I find myself having to depend upon them. I am grateful for their presence. I am thankful to have these strong foundations in my life. Help me to lean on them today as I take steps toward healing and wholeness. Amen.

THURSDAY
Breathing out

Read Genesis 18:1-8.

*The LORD appeared to Abraham by the oaks of
Mamre, as he sat at the entrance of his tent in the
heat of the day. He looked up and saw three men
standing near him.*

—Genesis 18:1-2

During a recent spiritual retreat, the leader invited me, along
with other group members, to participate in breath prayer.
In essence, this type of prayer consisted of breathing in and
out—deep, refreshing breaths meant to dispel fear, cleanse
the mind of distressing thoughts, and bring the body to a
place of serenity and peace. As we breathed in and out, the
leader invited us to whisper short prayers (hence, breath
prayers) of thanksgiving, recognition, and need. Or, as the
leader explained, we could also think of our breaths in as a
gift of God and our breaths out as our gift to others.

Perhaps you would find breath prayers helpful today.
They are simple, yes, but effective in bringing you to a still
place, a quiet place, a place of being.

As you breathe out, concentrate on the idea of your life
as a gift. You are gift to others. In fact, you may be offering
inspiration to your loved ones through your cancer journey.
Your courage and determination may serve as an example to
them. You may have friends who will see God's love through
your experiences and the way you face your fears.

Breathing out reminds you that even when you are ill, you
have much to give. You can offer hospitality and welcome—
just like Abraham welcomes the strangers into his home.

Had he not welcomed them, he would not have received their blessing: the promise of an heir.

Rest assured, God is still blessing you. God's promises still surround you. When you breathe out, you are offering the best of yourself, your gifts, your very life. Nothing separates you from the love of God.

Finally, as you breathe out, let go of any animosities, hurts, slights, or ill feelings toward others. Be your best self. Release any burdens from the past that might hinder your ability to face your diagnosis with confidence. Relinquish your fears and your anger. Releasing is not easy and may take time. But as you breathe, give your fear to God by saying, "I am afraid of _____." And as you release your anger, speak to God honestly and say, "I am angry because _____."

As you practice breath prayer—even if but for a few minutes a day—remember God's strength and faithfulness. Rely on this strength as you endeavor to embrace the wholeness of life that God wants for you.

Prayer

Lord of life, how wonderful is the world you have created! I am overwhelmed by your amazing grace. As I continue in my journey with cancer, help me to be aware that others may be watching me. Even through my illness, I can be a witness. I may be an inspiration to a friend, a child, or a family member. So as I breathe out today, grant me an awareness of your gifts and of how I can pass them on to others. Amen.

FRIDAY
Breathing in

Read Joel 2:28-29.

In those days, I will pour out my spirit.

—Joel 2:29

In Billy Graham's autobiography, the famed evangelist makes many references to his home in Montreat, North Carolina. In particular, Graham mentions a path on his property that he walked frequently. While walking on this path, he often composed sermons that he would later preach. The path itself was a method of prayer—a way of breathing in the inspiration of God.

Perhaps you have such a place in your life: a corner of tranquility, a comfortable chair, a picture window, a garden, a library. A familiar place can be one of the most inviting sanctuaries. Comfort enables us to relax, to be at one with God, and to find peace. In these places, we can breathe in the blessings of God and find new strength and insight.

I know some people who pray as they work in their gardens. Others have created prayer spaces in their bedrooms or dens. And still others enjoy a life of prayer by exercising outdoors—perhaps walking among flowers or in the woods. Some men I know claim that they feel a spiritual vitality on the golf course and actually consider the links a kind of church. Regardless of the space or place, people can create a daily ritual of accepting the blessings and promises that God has for them. You don't have to go far from home or enter great cathedrals to be at peace with God.

As you breathe in today while in the midst of your familiar surroundings, I hope you can release some of your anxieties, pain, and struggles to God. Breathing in reminds you that God has given you a new day—and with it many joys and triumphs.

As you read in the passage from the ancient Jewish prophet Joel, God pours God's Spirit over your life today and every day. When you take time to notice your own breathing and God's blessings, you may envision new paths or discover renewed energy. Feel God's leading in these moments; know that God has not forsaken you or left you to face your illness alone. There is hope.

Breathe in today, and take in the joy of your own existence. Give thanks for your blessings. And once you have recalled these reminders of God's love, seek a new strength for the day. You are still walking a difficult path, but you are not alone. God is with you.

Prayer

God above me, God around me, God within me: I thank you for the familiar today—for those places and moments that bring me great comfort. I think you for all the gifts—both large and small, unnamed and unknown—that you provide. Although I cannot name them all, I acknowledge that you are the Giver of all good things, and I praise you for these joys. Help me to receive what you would say to me this day, my strength and my Redeemer. Amen.

SATURDAY
Knowledge is strength

Read Proverbs 4:5-9.

Get wisdom; get insight; do not forget, nor turn away from the words of my mouth.

—Proverbs 4:5

Over the past twenty years, I have taught many writing courses. Although I am always busy working toward my own deadlines and goals for books, essays, and feature articles, helping other people with their writing projects has remained very important to me. I love the work and find it gratifying. Often, people in my writing classes will ask, "What should I write about?" The typical—even classical—answer is, "Write what you know."

But I, like many other writers of biographies, histories, and books of general interest, have always written about unfamiliar subjects. I find discovering new facts thrilling; I take joy in researching; I marvel at uncovering bits and pieces of histories and ideas. To me, this is what knowledge is—discovery. And in the end, knowledge is also strength.

Think back to your school days. No doubt you had a favorite subject or teacher. You experienced days when you discovered new ideas and, in turn, grew as a person (even if you were not aware of it). The changes and growth from learning are often imperceptible. But the knowledge you gained provided strength for your future pursuits.

Now fast-forward to your cancer journey. You may have already learned new facts and figures about your disease. You have done your homework. You have grown in your understanding. And through this learning, you have become stronger, even if you didn't perceive the differences right away. Your journey toward healing and wholeness will be made all the more robust as you increase your knowledge.

Give thanks today for what you have learned about cancer, about yourself, and about your family and loved ones. You may also have discovered a new faith and a deeper trust in God. Or you may simply have discovered the strength to rest in the care and expertise of others—even the very presence of God.

Knowledge is strength. And God will see you through.

Prayer

O God, I feel that I always have more to learn—and never enough time to learn it all. But I thank you for what others have taught me, and I appreciate the new insights I have gained on my cancer journey. I am not glad for the cancer, but I am thankful that I have discovered more about myself and about those I love. In this difficult time, may I also find opportunity to grow. Help me to rest in the assurance of your grace and loving-kindness. May gratitude fill my heart to overflowing. Amen.

SUNDAY
Looking to God

Read Psalm 121.

My help comes from the LORD,
who made heaven and earth.

—Psalm 121:2

In the Louvre Museum in Paris, France, people often stand in line for several hours for a distant glimpse of Leonardo da Vinci's *Mona Lisa*. But just around the corner from this famous painting hangs many other da Vinci works that, while painted by the same master's hand, draw far fewer crowds. Here, one can walk unencumbered and view da Vinci's works up close and personal.

One such da Vinci painting is *St. John the Baptist*. This interpretation of John presents him as a young man with soft features. His long, curly tresses lead the viewer's eyes toward John's outstretched hand, his long index finger pointing toward heaven.

We can almost hear John the Baptist saying, "Look to God." His finger points toward heaven, but his wry smile proclaims his assurance that God is good. Da Vinci managed to capture all this on canvas, just as the writer of Psalm 121 captures the marvel and mystery of God's abiding presence.

Centuries before da Vinci, the psalmist writes of looking toward the mountains—even beyond them—to the One who is highest of all: God, the Creator of the universe. The psalmist speaks of leaning on God for strength, assurance, and guidance. The psalmist shares the belief that since God created majestic mountains and the sun and moon, then surely God will care for God's children. Jesus may have had this psalm in mind when he says that God takes care of the sparrows and that we hold more value than they do. Jesus also notes that God makes the sun shine on the just and on the unjust alike. God acts without prejudice. God loves everyone. This is the very nature of God's grace.

Over the years, I have known people who have drawn strength from God in times of heartache and trouble. Leaning on God through uncertainties and fears can be difficult, but those who have kept their eyes on God have found themselves with a sense of deep trust.

Some months ago, my good friend Doug discovered God as his source of strength. For years, through various forms of cancer, treatment, and specialized care, Doug continued to lean upon God for his strength. He even kept his sense of humor through the tough times and was frequently the one who lifted up his wife and family when they fell into despair. I believe God gifted Doug not only with perseverance but also with unshakable hope.

Today, as you look to the Lord for your strength, take a lesson from the psalmist and consider God's creation. Notice the natural wonders—works of God that took, perhaps, centuries to complete. And you can rest assured that if God cares deeply for creation, God certainly cares for you.

Prayer

El Shaddai (God Almighty), I give you my heart and all my weaknesses. When I fall into despair, lift me up. When doubts arise, fill me with hope. Hold me in your mighty hand, and remind me of your abiding presence. I am safe in your arms. Bless me as I continue to place my faith and confidence in your loving power. Amen.

WEEK 3

Making a Plan & Leaning on Faith

MONDAY
Tough decisions

Read Philippians 2:12-18.

Do all things without murmuring and arguing.

—Philippians 2:14

Not long ago, I happened upon a published sermon with the title "Plan B." The sermon explored the many plans we create for ourselves, our families, and our futures. But as time goes by, we often discover that our best laid plans simply do not come to fruition. Likewise, our plans often become messy affairs, with many dead ends, roadblocks, and even confusion thrown into the mix.

A cancer diagnosis can certainly create an alternate course. No one expects to receive this news, and if you find yourself on the cancer journey, you may place your other plans on the back burner. You are forced to go to "Plan B."

The cancer trail is filled with many difficult decisions. In fact, you may have already been forced to make several. And through these tough choices, you have likely depended on God and the love of your family and friends.

As you continue to make the difficult decisions regarding your treatment and recovery, find solace in remembering that many others have faced tough choices too. Those who have lived before you have experienced doubt, fear, consternation, anxiety, and dread.

Consider the apostle Paul, for example. During his imprisonment, he writes several letters to churches—including his positive and uplifting letter to the church in Philippi. In that letter, Paul offers sage advice on approaching problems and decision-making. "Do all things without murmuring and arguing. . . . Be glad and rejoice with me" (Phil. 2:14, 18).

Of course, you may find taking Paul's advice when facing cancer to be difficult, but caregivers attest to this positive approach. Some years ago, during my chaplain residency, I recall a surgeon telling me, "Patients who have a positive outlook toward their recovery do so much better than those of a dour disposition." He went on to say that some surgeons would not perform an operation if a patient held a fatalistic outlook. "Attitude is vital," he said.

How true. And how important your attitude will be as you face the tough decisions ahead. Regardless of your prognosis or the many roadblocks you may encounter in the future, don't despair. Focus on those gifts that have blessed your life. Take the time to laugh each day. And if you find yourself struggling, surround yourself with positive, uplifting people and conversations.

"It is God who is at work in you" (Phil. 2:13), Paul writes to the people at Philippi. And God is at work within you too.

Prayer

Dear God, I have many tough decisions to make. Some of them weigh heavily on my mind. I turn to you because I need your power and strength. In the days ahead when I feel confused or anxious, I pray that you will give me the insights and direction I need. I know that you care for me in my weakness, that you understand suffering, and that you will hold me in your love. I trust in your everlasting care. Amen.

TUESDAY
Determination

Read Romans 8:31-39.

*What then are we to say about these things? If God is
for us, who is against us?*

—Romans 8:31

The sports industry is a big business. Communities love
their local sports teams, and people spend billions of dollars
annually on sports-related attire. Unfortunately, you don't
always hear those behind the scenes stories about triumph
and determination. You may not know about the dreams
and arduous journeys of many athletes who struggle to make
the team.

In sports, determination is a key factor in achieving any
goal, whether it be winning a single game or a national cham-
pionship. But determination is also required—perhaps even
in greater parts—across all walks of life, in all occupations,
and in everyday achievements.

Likewise, anyone who is making the arduous journey
through cancer will tell you that determination is a key factor
in the outcome. Determination is not just willpower but the
daily focus and attention to detail that make positive outcomes
possible. Determination is about staying the course, not giving
up, and holding out hope even when you are not at your best.

Years ago, when my friend Larry learned that he had a
cancerous growth on his esophagus, he became determined
to face his disease with hope and a plan. He talked to various
oncologists and surgeons, made his way through a maze of
options, and eventually settled on a treatment. Although his

prognosis was not stellar, Larry beat the odds. Twelve years later, he is living a full and healthy life.

I have known many other people who have had similar outcomes despite the odds. All of them noted determination as an important factor in their healing.

The scriptures never hide life's difficulties, but they point toward the importance of faith, hope, and love. In life, you are called to "press on" toward life's highest aspirations, toward the goals and blessings God has in store for you. You certainly need God's strength and grace, but you also need determination, perseverance, and faith.

As you consider the goals that lie before you in your cancer journey, you may encounter days when you feel weak or discouraged. That doesn't mean you lack determination. No one—not even a top athlete—can perform at an optimal 100-percent level every day. And your cancer goals may look different than someone else's. Some cancer patients experience physical healing; some do not. Your goal may be remaining hopeful in times of grief, enjoying moments with family and friends, experiencing pain-free days, or celebrating a final chemotherapy treatment.

Whenever you do feel weak or discouraged, don't despair. God is with you. As the psalmist writes, "God is our refuge and strength, a very present help in trouble" (Ps. 46:1). God is the true source of your determination.

Prayer

O God, I may not be able to see the finish line right now, but I will continue to press on. Thank you for your amazing grace that has sustained me and given me hope. I am blessed to call you friend, counselor, guide, helper, and Savior. Help me to receive and appreciate your gifts this day. Amen.

WEDNESDAY
Confidence

Read Psalm 89:1-8.

*I declare that your steadfast love is established forever;
your faithfulness is as firm as the heavens.*

—Psalm 89:2

When our children were younger, my wife and I noted that they both lacked self-confidence. This lack of confidence showed up in their academic work as well as in their extracurricular activities. My wife and I made a point to instill more confidence in our children as they grew older, but we also wanted them to have confidence in others and in the greater forces that were at work in their lives.

Confidence is an important ingredient in life. The confidence that you feel in yourself and in others can be life-changing. In many respects, confidence is faith.

People define faith in different ways, of course. When I was younger, I thought of faith as intellectual assent to a particular set of beliefs. Later, faith became trust. And now, even later in my life, faith is my strong and unwavering confidence in God.

You may consider your cancer journey to be a path toward increasing your confidence. You need to have confidence in the physicians, in the nursing staff, and in those who administer your treatments. Likewise, you must have confidence in the abilities of surgeons or even the quality of care that you will receive.

Eventually your confidence may manifest itself as an ultimate trust in God. This is the faith of which the psalmist speaks, and this faith has the power to enliven your heart, open your mind, and instill in you a hope for the future. Confidence is important to your well-being and to your ability to believe the best about tomorrow.

As you consider your own cancer journey, take a moment to reflect on the importance of confidence. In whom have you placed your trust? For what do you hope? How have others added to your level of confidence?

Prayer

My heavenly Father, thank you for the joy of trusting in you. I know I do not have all of the answers to life's questions; I still have much to learn. But I will place my confidence in the assurance of your grace. If I slip and fall, I know you will pick me up. Open my eyes and heart that I may see the blessings you have in store for me today. Amen.

THURSDAY
Perseverance

Read 1 Timothy 6:11-16.

Fight the good fight of the faith.

—1 Timothy 6:12

Many biblical narratives speak to the mystery and blessings of long life. The lives of Abraham and Sarah come to mind, as does the saga of Jacob's sons and the life of Joseph. The psalmist writes of "threescore years and ten" (90:10, KJV), and the New Testament writers—especially the writer of Acts—leave the impression that most of the apostles lived to ripe old ages. One common theme throughout, however, is the idea of perseverance.

In fact, perseverance was deemed such an important ingredient of Christian faith that many creeds were written with the understanding that the faithful continue on their paths—even in the face of overwhelming odds. In his letters, the apostle Paul exhorts fellow believers to persevere.

No doubt you have also experienced moments when you exhibited perseverance—with your family, in your work, and in your varied pursuits when you have stayed the course, continued, and not given up. And when it comes to facing a cancer diagnosis with confidence, you know that perseverance is required. I compare perseverance to the active ingredients in medicine—it makes things happen.

Today, as you consider the challenges that are before you, remain steadfast in your resolve. Take a lesson from the leaders of old—from Abraham and Sarah, who were childless at an advanced age but believed in God's promise of a future. Or from the apostle Paul, who faced dangers and challenges at every turn and yet continued in his charge through hunger, threat, imprisonment, beatings, and overwhelming odds. You may know others who have persevered and won the day as well. And so can you.

Of course, perseverance is more than just grit or determination. Perseverance requires an attitude of action—a way of working and being involved in your redemption, growth, and change. As far as healing goes, the way of perseverance is not always easy, but it is essential. Proceed on your journey one day at a time, one step at a time. Perseverance is a gift. And all who practice it reap the rewards.

Prayer

Creator God, I am amazed when I consider your power that has created and is still creating the heavens and the earth. I know you continue to work in the universe, and you continue to work in me too. That is why I can persevere and why I need your strength. Days will come when I am weary, times when I may want to give up. But if you lead me, I know I will find a way to overcome. Guide me, Lord. Amen.

FRIDAY
The power of prayer

Read Psalm 23.

The LORD is my shepherd, I shall not want.

—Psalm 23:1

The Psalms are often described as the prayer book of the Bible. These varied Psalms—all 150 of them—describe many types of prayer. Some psalms are corporate—sung by the multitudes as they entered the temple for worship. Other prayers are deeply personal—reflecting individual needs, laments, confessions, hatreds, or thanksgivings. And still others contain wonderfully powerful metaphors and poetic expressions filled with wonder and delight.

Psalm 23—perhaps the most well-known and widely used of all the Psalms—has offered comfort and meaning to people for centuries. Though often read at funeral services, the Twenty-third Psalm is actually for the living, a prayer of hope for the new day.

Psalm 23 reminds me that prayer is a powerful tool. Prayer is personal but also simple in expression and filled with gratitude and need. You can even use this psalm as an exemplar for prayer, noting that it contains the following components:

> a personal address to God (How would you address God today?)
>
> an expression of need (What do you need today?)
>
> an acknowledgment of God's blessings (Where/ how has God blessed you?)

an acknowledgment of God's leading (Where is God leading you now?)

a personal expression of your fears (What do you fear?)

a final expression of gratitude (For what or whom are you thankful?)

Psalm 23 is beautiful, but it is no more beautiful than any prayer that you can write yourself. You can even pray the psalm itself (as I frequently do). Your prayers hold marvelous power. Consider the elements of Psalm 23 now as you write your own prayer. Through prayer, you will strengthen your relationship with God.

Prayer

Pray your prayer based on Psalm 23.

SATURDAY
Second wind

Read Psalm 66.

Make a joyful noise to God, all the earth.

—Psalm 66:1

My wife and I have always loved to hike, but we are now more aware of our advancing ages during physical activity. On a trip to Boulder, Colorado, we decided to hike a mountain trail marked "moderate." We initially thought the climb would take one hour and provide a leisurely walk. But the trail, we soon discovered, was an arduous trek. Some portions of the trail had washed away, and large boulders blocked other sections. What we thought would be a one-hour hike turned into a four-hour journey. At many junctures along the way, we had to stop and catch our breath as we climbed to the top of the mountain.

My wife and I noted, however, that we each received a "second wind"—a point when we knew we could make it to the top and press on through our discomfort. The second wind provided a shot of energy and focus.

My wife also experienced this second wind following her surgery for breast cancer. At points in her cancer journey, she sensed that she was going to make a full recovery.

Regardless of where you are on your own path with cancer, focus your prayer today on receiving that second wind—a refreshing outpouring of God's spirit. You may picture wind catching your sails or consider a majestic bird—an eagle, perhaps—soaring over a landscape. Be encouraged by the words of the prophet Isaiah: "Those who wait for the LORD shall renew their strength, they shall mount up with wings like eagles, they shall run and not be weary, they shall walk and not faint" (40:31). You may discover that today is a turning point in your battle with cancer.

Seek refreshment today: plan an outing with your family, arrange a picnic, read a good book, spend time with a favorite hobby, call a friend, eat at your favorite restaurant.

Today is your second wind. Today is the beginning of your new life.

Prayer

Holy God, you have given me what I needed in these weeks past, and I know I have grace-filled days ahead of me. Refresh me with hope, joy, and love today. May the words of my mouth and the meditations of my heart be acceptable to you this day, my strength and my Redeemer. Amen.

SUNDAY
Running the race

Read Hebrews 12:1-3.

Since we are surrounded by so great a cloud of witnesses, let us also lay aside every weight and the sin that clings so closely, and let us run with perseverance the race that is set before us.

—Hebrews 12:1

When my friend Doug was diagnosed with cancer, he noted that his first month with the disease felt like a sprint. "It seemed like I was making a decision every day," he told me. "But after my first round of chemo treatments went well, I found myself living at a different pace. For the next three years, I was in and out of treatments, and then I felt like I was running a marathon."

Many cancer patients describe their journey as a type of race. Some describe the journey in hurried cadences, while others speak of the long, protracted walk through weeks and years. Depending upon your prognosis, type of cancer, and type of treatments, this journey can seem like a sprint over a smooth, flat surface or a cross-country competition across a varied landscape.

When the writer of Hebrews describes the "cloud of witnesses" and the "race that is set before us," he offers a deep theological affirmation about the nature of the church. You cannot, after all, forget that people of faith have come before you. You are not the first person to hurt; to experience difficulties, setbacks, and injuries. Rather, you must place your sufferings within the context of history. This history—including those who have lived before you and persevered—is full of affirmation and examples of faith and fortitude. The writer of Hebrews reminds you to look toward the past for glimpses of others' healing and redemption.

You can find these comforts in a variety of ways. You may consider your own family history and take note of the inspirational guides who made their way through this world. Or you may seek those who are still running their races. In their faith, you may find a living witness of God's presence and love. Either way, this knowledge can help you to run your own race with cancer.

The race, of course, is never easy. But it is worth the effort. Always.

Prayer

Dear Lord, I am still running my race, but I know you have given me the energy and tools I need to make my way across the finish line. May I always seek your guidance. Continue to bless me in my journey, and encourage me when I feel like giving up. O God, I pray that my gratitude will be evident through my life and words this day. Amen.

WEEK 4

Hope & Healing

MONDAY
Embracing change

Read 1 Peter 3:6-18.

Christ also suffered for sins once for all, the righteous for the unrighteous, in order to bring you to God.

—1 Peter 3:18

During the years I knew Margie, she always seemed to be battling cancer. But one day she received word from her doctor that her cancer was in remission. When I visited her at home, however, she seemed rather depressed. I asked her to explain.

"During these months that I've been sick, I have been on the receiving end of so much love and attention. People have called, brought food by the house, sent cards, and have even taken me to my chemo appointments. But now I realize that all of that will be gone. It's difficult to think about what being healthy means to me now."

Like Margie, I have known many others who felt depressed after receiving good news about their health. But Margie's explanation made sense to me. If someone has been sick for months and received so much love and attention, what happens when that daily support and care goes away? For Margie, good news was not easy news. Good news came with its own set of responsibilities, dreams, and life changes.

As you have read through this book, I hope that you have made prayerful decisions about your treatment. I also hope that you have received good news about your prognosis. If you have not received good news, I hope that you have heard words of comfort and support and biblical guidance that may ease your fears and help you move toward the peace that Jesus offers. Even in the midst of uncertainty and fear, I pray that God's great love will hold you and offer meaning to each day.

Take a few minutes today to consider the good that has transpired in your cancer journey so far. Where have you felt God's care? How have you been blessed by the prayers and gifts of others? Remembering these blessings will help you embrace the changes that come with renewed or declining health. Ask your family and friends to help you handle the changes—whether good or bad—in your life. God will be there to empower you and direct you as well.

Prayer

God of healing and salvation, I am nothing without you. I am thankful that you work your miracles within me. I am fearfully and wonderfully made. I pray that joy and gratitude may be evident in my life—through my words and actions— as I step out in faith to embrace the new path that is before me. Amen.

TUESDAY
Difference-makers

Read Matthew 5:1-10.

Blessed are the poor in spirit, for theirs is the kingdom of heaven.

—Matthew 5:3

You and I live in a disposable world. Most everything you buy—from washers and dryers, to automobiles and toasters—is designed to eventually wear out. This disposable mentality has shaped consumerism in innumerable ways—even to the point that the word *disposable* is printed on certain products.

Sadly, this broken world also regards human beings in much the same fashion. Throughout history, holocausts, ethnic cleansing, and many other atrocities have been committed that have essentially cast people under the banner of disposable. And your own mortality—brought to the forefront of your mind when you have a serious illness—can make you feel very disposable too.

But Jesus never treats people as if they are disposable. In fact, he sees others as indisposable, invaluable treasures designed by God. And that's what you are.

Jesus also teaches that each person can make a difference in the world. You have a purpose, and you have gifts to share. Though you may struggle to find God in the midst of your suffering, rest assured that God sees you as a unique being who adds value to the world God created.

As you have made this journey through cancer—even thus far—no doubt you have learned much about yourself and about your purpose and dreams. You have probably prayed, wept, worried, and wondered. You may have experienced days of anxiety and despair as well as days of enormous joy.

But I'm here to tell you that God created you to be a difference-maker. Jesus teaches this in many ways. As Jesus says, you are salt of the earth. You are light of the world. You are one whose spirit can soar and make the kingdom of heaven real to others.

Consider your life today. Who are you impacting with your actions? How can you share your spirit with others? What words of hope can you speak to those in dire situations? How can you pray, serve, and love?

You can be a difference-maker to many people, and through your experience with cancer, you can demonstrate the resiliency of the human spirit and the significance of faith. You can offer your testimony—facing cancer with bravery and conviction—as a gift to others.

Don't doubt the difference you can make in others' lives. Let your light shine.

Prayer

Gracious God, I am humbled by my experiences with cancer, and I pray that my life can be a testimony to your grace. Thank you for my doctors, oncologists, and surgeons; thank you for my family and friends. Thank you for the opportunities to serve you and others—perhaps fellow cancer patients making their own journeys. Grant me your peace this day, and shower your peace upon others. Amen.

WEDNESDAY
Healing touch

Read Psalm 41.

O LORD, be gracious to me.

—Psalm 41:10

People turn to the Psalms during times of trouble because of their honesty and their ability to speak into everyday situations and struggles. While some are corporate prayers—even worshipful in tone and content—others, such as Psalm 41, are deeply personal. In the context of cancer, Psalm 41 reads like a contemporary prayer—insightful and filled with emotion and grit.

While visiting my friend Bob, who was undergoing a fourth round of chemo, I happened upon a small concrete plaque near his front steps. In the shape of a hand, the plaque contained a prayer for God's healing touch and abiding presence. I learned that friends had placed this concrete plaque near Bob's front steps as a tangible reminder of God's blessing—a way of saying, "God's hand is upon you."

I have thought about that plaque many times since my visit and considered all the ways that hands express emotions. A clenched fist shows anger. An open, outstretched hand offers a sign of welcome or vulnerability. An upraised hand may mean stop. A hand placed on someone's shoulder can be more powerful than a spoken prayer. My hands can bless or curse, take or receive. I can use them to feed myself or others. Hands convey the feelings of the heart.

Where have you felt the touch of God's hand in your cancer journey? You may have felt God during your struggles or your victories, during the quietness of resignation or the joy of good news. You may have felt God's touch through the hands of others—those who have helped you, those who have written encouraging notes, or those who were in charge of your medical care. Consider how you have been touched by God in recent days. How can you use your hands to convey warmth and healing to those around you? Your hands can be your own personal psalm.

Trust your hands. Let them speak for you. And trust that God will continue to touch you as well—a healing touch that will bless, preserve, and keep you now and forever.

Prayer

O Lord, thank you for your warm and giving touch in my life. I know that you have placed your hand upon me, and I have felt your strength in my time of need. Allow me to be your hands for someone else today. Help me to use my hands to bless others. May today be a day of both receiving and giving. Amen.

THURSDAY
Friends and family

Read Psalm 42.

> *By day the LORD commands his steadfast love,*
> *and at night his song is with me,*
> *a prayer to the God of my life.*

—Psalm 42:8

My grandmother used to have a small, embroidered wall-plaque in the kitchen bearing the following words: *Make new friends, but keep the old. One is silver, and the other gold.* I've realized the truth of these words countless times in my life. In the aftermath of my wife's breast cancer diagnosis, she and I often gave thanks for the incredible gift of friendship and took solace in that adage's truth.

Scripture affirms the blessings of friendship time and again. Isolation, loneliness, despair—loving and caring relationships trump these feelings. Many psalms speak to the abundant joy found in human connection.

During my thirty-five years of pastoral ministry, I have often reminded people (especially in times of need) that God not only created them as individuals but also as part of a community. Even in the Bible, lone figures are joined by listeners, followers, helpers, and community in due time. Community expands as understanding, love, and creativity is enjoyed.

As I consider my own life, I see that I have been blessed by my connections with others. During my childhood, I had many friends, and when I traveled out of state for college, I discovered a new cadre of compatriots despite my naturally introverted personality. Over the course of my life, I have ministered to more than ten thousand people, and I must say that the church has been very good to me and my family. In short, nothing in my life has been achieved in a pure state of individual effort—there have always been others in my court, supporting me, coaching me, and cheering me on.

As you consider your blessings of family and friends, I know you will arrive at the same conclusion. Your community—unique and sacred as it is—has lifted you during your cancer journey in innumerable ways. God's people have been there for you. That's just the way God works.

Take time today to give thanks for these special relationships and support systems. Name the ways these relationships have already brought healing into your life.

Prayer

God of family and friendship—thank you for giving me the gift of relationship. I can see your grace through the love shown to me and the love I've shown others. The tender care of others reminds me of your tender care. I give thanks for all my loved ones and offer them to you, heavenly Father. Amen.

FRIDAY
The new normal

Read Psalm 48.

[God] will be our guide forever.

—Psalm 48:14

As a young child, I thought that every family mirrored my own. Only later in my life did I realize that not all families contained two parents, a sibling, and a slew of uncles, aunts, and cousins. As a teen, I assumed that everyone aspired to the same goals that I did. And even now as an adult, I find it difficult to accept differences in certain individuals and situations. But what I consider to be normal may not be normal for someone else.

No doubt, your cancer experience has included some unsavory and abnormal days. Your new normal may include sitting in a chemo waiting room or lying on a bed during a radiation treatment. Your new normal may also include frequent trips to the pharmacy or more frequent prayers. And over time, you may have settled into this new way of life— this new course for the day.

A year after my wife's breast cancer diagnosis, she discovered that her new normal looked very different from her old life. Her heart told her to take a new path—to discover a new way of life in the aftermath of her recovery. Many people who have endured and survived a traumatic experience with cancer also reach this conclusion. A return to normal doesn't always mean a return to the way life was before the diagnosis.

Some people, in fact, make career changes postcancer. Others experience a spiritual awakening or discover a deeper devotion to their families and friends. Your life may have changed in many ways, but consider how you can allow a sense of normalcy to return to your life. Your new normal may involve a reinstatement of old routines. Or it may consist of newfound joys and opportunities. Make a list of old joys you are excited to bring back into your life. Follow that list with one of new experiences you want to try.

Prayer

Dear God, I am grateful for the ways my life is returning to the familiar, the cherished, the normal. I know that certain aspects of my life will never be the same, but even the hardest experiences in my cancer journey have provided insight and learning. I am now ready to face life afresh, honoring the return of old routines and relishing newfound joys. Bless me, I pray, with wisdom, direction, and fortitude as I face this new future. Amen.

SATURDAY
Gratitude

Read Psalm 145.

Great is the LORD, and greatly to be praised.

—Psalm 145:3

Many years ago, I served as the guest speaker at a corporate event. After my talk, the company's executive escorted me back to his office where I noticed an open file drawer stuffed with an array of greeting cards, letters, and stationery. "What's that?" I asked.

"That's my affirmation file," the executive told me.

I asked him to explain.

"Did you know," he said, "that whenever people receive a critical comment, they tend to fixate upon the negative? And did you know that psychologists say that it takes ten positive comments to outweigh a negative one?"

"I didn't know that," I said. "But I can attest to its truth in my own life."

"That's why I keep my affirmation file," the executive explained. "I keep my birthday cards in there, positive feedback I receive, notes from colleagues, praises, things like that. And whenever I have a bad day, I take those positive affirmations out of their drawer and read them. That drawer keeps me balanced. It helps me recognize the positive in my life rather than the negative. Gratitude makes life worth living."

Ever since that conversation, I have kept an affirmation file of my own. I have filled a desk drawer with positive notes, cards, and letters that uplift me.

I wholeheartedly encourage you to make an affirmation file as well. Instead of throwing away those cards and letters you've received during your cancer journey, keep them. Let them be a source of encouragement and gratitude for the years ahead. They will remind you of how far you have come and the many blessings you have received from God.

Gratitude is one of the most powerful attitudes you can have in life. It is a force to be reckoned with. When you hold gratitude in your heart, you can face enormous changes and challenges with confidence and the calm assurance of God's guidance. Assume an attitude of gratitude and keep moving toward hope and healing, replaying positive conversations and remembering the love and care of others.

Prayer

O Lord, thank you for creating me with the capacity to care and the capacity to feel. Through my cancer journey, I have found new strength and reasons to be grateful. Allow me to show my gratitude in such a way that I will be a positive force and a help to others. Amen.

SUNDAY
Giving thanks

Read Psalm 150.

Praise the LORD!
Praise God in his sanctuary;
praise him in his mighty firmament!

—Psalm 150:1

As a child, your parents may have taught you the following magic words: *please* and *thank you*. The words *thank you*, of course, are closely tied to etiquette, but they embody so much more than good manners. Thank you—giving thanks—lies at the very heart of faith. In fact, throughout the scriptures, prophets and disciples express their thanks to God in times of difficulty and delight. The apostle Paul even goes so far as to suggest that people should give thanks in all circumstances.

As you have dealt with your cancer diagnosis, you have faced many highs and lows. You may have experienced days of despair followed by days of anticipation and elation. You may have encountered days of spirit-lagging sadness, only to be followed by days of gratitude.

As you have read through this book, you have filled your journey with prayer. I hope you have found care and support in both familiar and unfamiliar places and learned the value of giving thanks each day.

At the end of my wife's cancer journey, she found herself wanting to write thank-you notes to an array of people—persons who had become very special to her. Writing those notes served as another form of therapy for her. Likewise, the need to express thanks is just another step in the healing process.

Your list of thanksgivings may not be lengthy—or it could be overwhelmingly long. Either way, take a few moments today to offer your thanks to God. This prayer does not need to be filled with flowery language or rote words; this prayer just needs to come from your heart.

The final psalm in the Bible offers a hymn of thanks. How fitting to end the Psalms—filled with grievances, laments, and heartache—with gratitude, one of the most important ingredients of faith. Gratitude evokes a joy that unites you to your Creator and fills you with new appreciation for life.

Don't let today slip away without offering thanks for your family and support network, for your friends, for your physicians and therapists. And thanks be to God, the Giver of all good gifts.

Prayer

O God, how do I express my thanks? My words seem inadequate. Still, I pray that you will receive my appreciation as I consider your goodness toward me. Your grace is sufficient, and I owe my life to you. Amen.

REFLECTION QUESTIONS

These questions are designed to stimulate further reflection for individuals or small groups. I suggest reviewing each week's meditations before answering these questions.

Week 1: Speaking of Cancer & Overcoming Shock

1. What feelings best describe your thoughts about your situation right now? What would you like to express to others?

2. What past experiences (especially difficulties) serve to remind you of God's abiding presence? How can you best focus on God's promises?

3. If you were to make a list of three things you need most right now, what would be on it?

4. Where might you best focus your energies today as you seek God's healing?

5. What stresses and cares do you need to release from your life today?

6. What goals inspire you to seek wholeness? What steps do you need to take to face your fears?

7. Over the past week, what three experiences stand out as positive and uplifting? How can these embolden you to continue your journey with confidence?

Week 2: Making Decisions & Learning Again

1. How would you describe your learning style? What have you learned about cancer that will help you heal?

2. Where do you need to focus your attention today in order to feel affirmed and hopeful?

3. How might you express your needs to others?

4. What pastimes or techniques can help you relax?

5. How are you nurturing your spirit? How can you exercise your faith?

6. What three things have you learned about cancer in the past week?

7. What Bible verses offer you the most comfort? (Write them down, and keep them handy in the days ahead.)

Week 3: Making a Plan & Leaning on Faith

1. What anxieties and cares do you need to give over to God this week?

2. If you could write a letter to God describing your future goals postcancer, what would the letter say?

3. What successes in your past have given you confidence? How can you draw upon these to embrace the future with a new confidence?

4. How are your relationships helping you move forward in your faith? Name five ways.

5. If you created a Top 10 list of blessings, what would be on it?

6. When your spirit feels faint, what thoughts provide new energy?

7. What do you need to do today to embrace your cancer journey with new enthusiasm and determination?

Week 4: Hope & Healing

1. What changes have you experienced since being diagnosed with cancer? How have they shaped your life?

2. Who has made a difference in your cancer journey?

3. How would you describe God's healing to others?

4. What do you appreciate most about your family and friends?

5. What aspects of your new normal are most appealing to you?

6. How can you express gratitude to others today?

7. In your own words, how would you thank God for the gift of life and the blessings you have known?

ABOUT THE AUTHOR

Todd Outcalt is a United Methodist pastor of thirty-five years who has authored more than thirty books in six languages, including *The Other Jesus: Stories from World Religions* (Rowman & Littlefield), *The Best Things in Life Are Free: Cherishing the Simple Pleasures* (Faith Communications), *Common Ground: Lessons and Legends from the World's Great Faiths* (Skyhorse), and *Husband's Guide to Breast Cancer: A Complete & Concise Plan for Every Stage* (Blue River Press). He also has a poetry collection, *Where in the World We Meet* (Chatter House Press). He has written eight books for Abingdon Press and also has written widely on the cancer experience for such national magazines as *Cure*, *The Barefoot Review*, *Together*, and *The Way of St. Francis*, from whom he received the Simon Scanlon Prize for his essay "The Stigmata and the Breast." His book *The Healing Touch: Experiencing God's Love in the Midst of Our Pain* has been used by cancer support groups around the country and has been translated into Polish.